Sugarcane

By Liana English

Special thanks

To Mom
For being kind enough to pick up the pieces,
of my shattered heart.
For being patient enough to help me glue them back together.
When no one else
Cared

To Dad
You Know

&

To Family
Love comes in different forms
I truly appreciate yours

Most importantly,
Thank God
For Ability
And Strength
Through what I thought I couldn't win

- Romans 1:16

Sugarcane

"You want people to believe you are a sunrise
I still hear the signs
No need to tell lies
I can see it in your eyes
That you fail to realize
That a "sunset" is just as *beautiful*"

Sugarcane

Contents

Sugarcane

Welcome

*Never Forget You Are
Worth More Than You
Know*

Sugarcane

Welcome to my storytime
I'm Sugarcane
With nectar in my eyes
And honey in my veins
My mouth drips many flavors
That some favor
Yes, some dislike
I've cried sweet tears at night
The tears only came to pass
And I remind myself of the honeycombs
That I have
The ones who stay indulge
In my sugarcane
It gets in their eyes
Blinded by the sugar night
They no longer see the stars that are bright
They expect me to be a bakery
With doughnuts, cakes, and whatever it makes
That they forget that I'm Sugarcane
With honey in my veins
I don't have all of the ingredients
To make the bakery of their imaginations
They try to put me on their plantations
Of expectations
They tell me I'm not trying hard enough
When I don't make the dessert of their dreams
But in reality, they are just
Blinded from me.

Sugarcane

The pages that you turn from right to left
Starts with the beginning of me
To what I've learned to invest
The quoted tattoos on the pages
Are the flavors from off of my tongue
You'll learn how the Sugarcane
Earned honey veins
Going through *Life* into the *Lessons* I've *Learned*
I've learned how not to burn
Because I'm not going down that road anymore…

Sugarcane

Life
Honey Drips

When my mouth can't explain
The feelings I have
My heart
Writes it down
It spills all of the emotions it has
Flooding a page as it overflows
To the next
Writing for hours
My heart to the page
My mouth has nothing
To say

Sugarcane

The rain falls from the clouds
And splats on the ground
It has no choice at all but to fall
It has no favor in where it lands
It can be good, bad, or drown in the sands
But its whole purpose is to water the land

Sugarcane

I sit at a table with many words around me
The words waterfall off of the lips of many
And pool into an ocean of conversation
The ocean is pure with laughter and clear with
kindness
One person's lie
Like a bucket of ink
Spills off of their lips
Down the waterfall into the ocean of conversation
Polluting and causing destruction in the ocean
Because of this
Relationships become extinct

Sugarcane

Trouble,
Why are you here?
I can feel your lies and presence in the air
So much anger and tears make a river
It's hard not to quiver
No one knows how you began
But the one who milked the cow
Sits quietly with happiness in her brow
Eating popcorn with the opposite of a frown
                    As she is the least expected…

People like to
Try
And paint inside of my hive
Search to see what they can find
In My Hive
Steal
From My Hive
Pick blemishes out
Of My Hive
But If you look
Deep down inside
You'll find
That they *can't* even find the key to their *own* **hive**

I feel misunderstood
When I speak
I'm heard
But no one listens
When I laugh
They hear thunder
When I smile they see weakness
When I express my thoughts
People began to widen their vocabulary
Are They Intimidated?
My inner intentions are a hill of sugar
But
I'm treated as if it's Mount Everest
Maybe I'm misunderstood
Or maybe
I'm a bird
In a leap of leopards

Sugarcane

I have pores that can lead to my spirit
It's common but it can lead deep down
While it's there it can corrupt
                        Thoughts
                        Emotions
                        It drinks that sap
                        It feels like a slap
We all have holes that lead to our spirit
A pit in our body
Through our ears, eyes,
and places that are naughty
Try to guard your holes with glue
Even a snare can trap you

Feeling numb on the inside
"I'm fine"
Is my welcome sign
That sits in front of my hive
As I dive into what hides
I say I'm fine to wrap what's mine

Sugarcane

When darkness covers the sky above
Is when my dove comes alive
I close my eyes my dreams arrive
I write what I see
Until my words touch the sky
The moon is the light that
Guides my hand as the pages fill
And my heart heals

Sugarcane

Some, have people they miss
Some only miss memories
But I miss the essence of your heart
Not the bombs on the mountain you climb
My heart misses the covering
And the song that you rhyme
But my spirit didn't like
Your troubles on the inside
The day came
To choose between my spirit
And my heart
My spirit won
But my heart cries

Have You Watched The News?
The flu of anger is becoming very contagious
The only cure is inside of the person themselves
This flu
Is different from any other flu,
Because it can be
Addicting
I realized this flu was in my household
When I was only a child
My father caught it
It consumed him
Capturing the very *soul* of the person he
could've been.
Now he's contagious
I try to stay away from his flu
Although,
Sometimes I sneeze it hasn't, it won't, destroy me,
    I have a cure
    I Am The Cure
    For Myself

I can feel the radiation
That comes from you
Through my body into
My heart
Even when you are not present
Your radiation still lingers

- As if you never left

She would not be chasing
What she
Thinks
She is missing
If someone gave her
What she needed

-*What she <u>thought</u> she needed*

Sugarcane

You are a mountain
You feel the sun beaming down
You believe your exhale creates the clouds
You feel the wind flowing out
When *we* get flooded <u>you</u> stand out
In your height, you see no one else
But the reality is we are all on the same
grounds

Sugarcane

A destination of attraction
That many flock to admire
Believed to be a high-standard
By strangers
Acquaintances
But when you come close
You'll see
That the envy is only a mirage

Few snakes can camouflage their scales
To be
Whatever enchants the thinking
Those who thrill the unknown
Love a mirage to envy
The reality of a person who fakes

Those who are indulged
Won't believe
Their eyes
They will reject *your yells*
To believe the
Lie
Of the mirage

Standing in front of a mirror
You do not reflect yourself
You are someone else
You try a conversation that will capture my being
But it falls to the ground
Because I know its true meaning
I can see you even though the mirror can't
I see the shadow that it doesn't reflect
It follows you around
I see what you are
You are not you
The shadow is who you are

Sugarcane

He,
Fell in love with the words that
I spoke
But he didn't know me for me
That's why we broke

In an art gallery
People walk and people talk
Few mock
Some point, others feel the art in their joints
Some admire, others tire
But most of all they judge the empire
They judge it by what they see,
Not by what it may be.
No one considers how the artist felt at the time
Or the rhyme that makes it chime
The birth of it's worth
People judge what they see and feel
They don't consider what is real

Sugarcane

Stamping the ink of my thoughts
On a page
Tattooing the pages
The ink from my cup is emptying
Becoming lighter in weight
&
My pages are becoming full

Trust can be painful
When it dives into
A person in disguise
Who suck you dry
Leaving you with tears in your eyes
Without a reason why

- Be Careful Who You Trust

Tight put together
Uplift one another
Forever
The words you speak lift me off my feet
Promises
Of the beauty we created
Glued together
Friends forever
But at the end of the day
You're the last to clap at my
Parade...

- Were we ever friends?

I see so many fake people
That fake becomes familiar
Familiar becomes fake
Can You Tell Salt From Sugar,
Just By Looking At It?
Can You Detect Unscented Toxic
Gas In Common Air?
Can You Taste Drugs In Vodka?

-College

The little girl wanted to believe
The words of a
"Friend"
She wanted to trust a friend
Until the end
She was trying to fill a void
With the company of someone else
Her cheese was easy to melt
They knew what she felt
That's why they picked her and
No one else
They broke her heart
That's how she felt
But little did she know
Her spirit never left

I was young, careless,
Naïve
My book came open
For all to see
Though they couldn't read far
The chapters they could see
They wrote their own story
In me
About me
And they read it to
Me
My first chapters
I was no longer the author of

-Learning to close my book

Sugarcane

Some come to the doorstep
With gifts of love
But it's **not** easy for me to open the door
When I recently had a burglary

You are a Zebra
She is a Lion
You are afraid of her
Naturally
She is the predator
You are the prey
You saw her consume
Your friends
You
Are intimidated
But you are also blinded
By your fear
If you could see
You would notice her
Power is also her *Weakness*
It lives in her jaw
A Zebra's (your) kick is **Powerful**
It'll easily break her jaw
She would Die from Starvation
You Would Win.
Strategize
Use your words
They Are Your Kick

Look into the distance
You'll see the beauty.
Orange on the mountains
Many speak of the time they traveled there
But the land is untouched...
Rumors
About what it could be,
Flowers?
Chemical reactions?
The earth's light or reflection?
Believing the storytellers
That the mountain was laced in beauty
No one adventured to see
What the orange light could be…

Sugarcane

As a child, with puberty roaring under my skin,
I walked into a beautiful house.
I wandered into the kitchen,
there are many familiar faces,
they all give me a flower then quickly
ignored my presence...
Confused, I kept the flowers
but I walked into a different room,
I heard a conversation flowing down the hall.
I entered the room in hope to join the conversation,
when I entered,
the conversation stopped
and there was no one present.
I noticed the pattern,
I dropped the flowers and
I decided to leave the house.
A photo flies through a window capturing
my attention, it's a photo of the people
I know and love, having fun, without me...
A man came and hugged me from behind,
he whispered "My name is Loneliness".

Loneliness took it upon himself to follow me uninvited.
After a few years, Loneliness continued to
 follow my every step, one day
I decided to confront him. I growled,
"Why are you here? Stop following me!"
I began to cry "Leave me alone! It's been too long,
LET ME LIVE" He Replied Simply, "Look Around You"
I did as I was told, but I saw no one *just me*.
"What do you want from me?" I asked.
He answered, "Look Closer At Each Person Who Left" I
looked around, I saw confusion amongst my family.
Lies spread across a group of friends, poisoning their
hearts. Depression sickening some,
while anger sacrificed others.
Best friends became perfect enemies.
Envy, and competition
poisonous people in the form of flower gardens. I found
tears driving pain into a crash a revenge. That's when I
realized, I wasn't being rejected...
I was being **protected.**

"Now That You Are On The Outside Of Them,
You Can See Them For Who They Really Are"
-Loneliness

Sugarcane

As the number of years grow
Close friends become
Strangers
As the number of years grow
You become wiser to
Danger
As the number of years grow
You separate from some of the people you
Know
The strongest plant can still grow on
Its own

Sugarcane

I need to go to bed
Not me
The thoughts in my head
The thoughts about the errands I haven't run
Or the things that are undone
What I should've done
What I could've done
What I would've said
Sometimes I feel like I'm trapped
In life's worrying sap
I need to take a nap
To get away from this crap
I won't give up or snap
Sometimes I just want to reset my map

Sugarcane

I have so many thoughts in my head,
So many emotions in my heart,
So many memories to forget,
So many words to express,
That it no longer fits through my mouth

It's easy to hold water
It's more difficult to drink it
When water is poured into your hand
You drink it
Nourishing the body
But
Sometimes it's easy to hold the water
In your hands
Without drinking it
So you have nourishment
But
It's slowly leaking out of the cracks
Of your fingers

You can't fix a broken heart
With the word "sorry"
Can you fix a shattered vase
With tape?

Dear Naysayers,
Dear Gossipers,
Dear Friends,
Dear Family,
Dear People,
Life Is Good,
You Should Try To Get Your Own

Sugarcane

The water and the land are separate
The ocean can only go so far
But then like love to the heart
The ocean can tsunami onto the land
Making a change that no one planned

Sugarcane

A popcorn kernel
Feeling the burn a little
Sitting in the heat
For what feels like hours
But then it flowers
Into a delightful treat to admire

Yes you can be alone in a room
With strangers *that you know*
Voices in the air
That you know are there
But you can't hear
There's no connection there
You try,
But they know you're different on the inside.
Like sitting in a church
That's religion isn't yours

Sugarcane

You hear the drum of the thunder
Thinking about the worries of life
The distractions from above
That you miss
The golden petals on the ground below

The wings in the air flow from your lips
They fly high in the air
I grasp them
I keep it in my heart
They carry ambition in their talons
Also a bit of joy, encouragement
I withhold it in my mind
I open my heart, emotions collide
A dove flies in the mist of the sky
These conversations are a prize

Does the sun know it shines brightly?
Does it know it's the primary for the existence of life?
When it rises, does it know it causes the day?
Does it know it is the eye of the sky while it is light?
When it sets does it know it kisses the sky with beauty?
When the stars arise at night
Do they know the twinkle in their eye
Is a picture in the sky?
Does the sky know it is the canvas where beauty is
placed?
Does it know without it, the planets would not look the
same?
Does it feel powerful when humans are amazed?
Maybe it is the same for you and for me,
Maybe,
We can't see what they see

First heartbreak

Picture

First love

Picture

Embarrassment

Picture

Terror

Picture

Sadness

Picture

Regret

Picture

Adventure

Picture

Amazement

Picture

Shame

Picture

Disappointment

Picture

Gratitude

Picture

Happiness

Picture

The photo album remains with you

Everywhere

-Our Minds Are A Camera

Sugarcane

Smile of a child
Is pure and mild
Though the seasons come and go
I can't let the forest overgrow the
The good memories
I do have

Sugarcane

It becomes easy
To walk on a dark path
And forget that you have a
Flashlight...
Search
You'll find the light

Thoughts spill off of
The imagination of a writer
Washing the emptiness off
Of the pages
Painting them with colorful words.
A reader
Can see their mind
Without meeting them
And hear their words
Without speaking

Sugarcane

It can be seen
But always felt
It devours a person inside out
It makes them feel like it is real
Without a doubt
It takes, it steals, it can even kill
But, perception is its weakness.
If your perception changes,
It'll kill it for ages
Because perception alters
Your reality

Lessons

Honey Sticks

Sugarcane

Spring births
The new beginnings of the earth
Its spirit fills the air
Causing teeth to shine everywhere
It's the beginning because
The unknown is near
When its birth develops
Summer isn't immature anymore

Summer captures warmth
Its beauty brings colorful grounds
The sun feels welcomed as it kisses the lands
The rain becomes a warm shower
When it waters the flowers
Seeds that were buried
Learn to uncover
Themselves
To be who they always
Were
Without any help
Happiness lives in the moments kept
As a new beginning *falls* into summer's steps

Fall is the only beauty in death
It proves when things fade away
There's something new in its steps...

Sugarcane

…The beauty of a chapter ending
Colors become vibrant as they fall into the past
One chapter can not always last
Many creatures begin to sleep away
But some will still stay awake
To see that beauty is also in simple things
As Winter spreads out its wings

Just because things are black and white
Doesn't mean beauty is out of sight
When the chilly nights
Sprinkles the earth with delight
The past-tense of creatures in the snow
They leave their signature in a row
Life remains underground
Sleeping until it hears the sound
Of a bird choir reuniting
Attracting the sun as it attends
The welcome of spring again.

Don't lose yourself to other people
Because
When you are lost
They will *not* be found

Sugarcane

Society knocked on my door today
It asked me, "If I wanted to come out and play?"
I asked it, "What games did you say?"
It said, "Role models and people to *portray*"
I told it, "I don't think that game is very fun"
And it said, "But it's for everyone"
I told society,
"I wasn't inclined, and I was a bit pressed for time"
Society said, "Not on my dime"
And it followed me every day,
Begging for me to come and play.
It started pointing out "problems" with my body,
Trying to make me feel like I'm "sorry."
It started showing me things,
How to "Perfect my body,"
Billboards,
Commercials,
Advertisements, GALORE
I said I wasn't interested, and it began to roar!
It placed before me a man who was a "high score."
The man told me to hide,
Unless I got a better backside,
At first, I examined my body,
To impress that hottie,
But then I told him to hide,
Because I'm not going to change in or outside.

Sugarcane

Society hit the floor and began to yell,
"Go die in a cell! You don't play very well!"
I'm not changing my life for someone else's grin,
I'm not knocking on a door, begging them to be let in,
I turned my back to society,
And told it to follow me,
Because you're not living YOUR life,
If you change under someone else's knife.

For your solace, I paid
For your friendship, I paid
For your food, I paid
For your shopping, I paid
For your happiness. I paid
For your travel, I paid
For your fun, I paid
For your family's smiles, I paid
For your emergencies, I paid
For your hope, I paid
Mercy, I paid
Chances, I paid
Peacefulness, I paid
For years I paid,
For all the lies you sold me
I fired the dealer,
and learned from my purchases...

Sugarcane

Walking down a path that never ends
A breeze of stress is weighing in
Strolling down a glass wall that will never pass
Frustration breaking glass
Dreaming of a dream that never dies
Seeing through blind eyes
Swimming up an endless stream
Silent scream
Procrastination standing before me

Sugarcane

The sun is waiting for you
You know what to do
But you stall
You see a crack in the wall
You search the crack to see
What it could be
You think your goals are in the hole
Especially when you see a little gold
Deep in the wall
Sleep is rising in your eyes
You still haven't found the prize
But when you awake
The sun has set
Your priorities haven't been met

A nail simply placed on a wall
Is a nail that falls
A nail that is improperly placed
Or rushed
Still falls from the wall
A nail that is hammered or drilled in a wall
Is a nail that is consistently sturdy
Hard work pays off
Other nails quickly placed
May not be sturdy

Sugarcane

She is sweet, she is mild
She is dainty, quiet
But oh, don't be fooled
She protects what she wants
She chooses her battles upfront
She is kind but also alert
She is the first to hear the "boom"
She is the "boom"
It's true silence and power can be in the same room

Sugarcane

You want people to believe you are a sunrise
I still hear the signs
No need to tell lies
I can see it in your eyes
That you fail to realize
That a "sunset" is just as *beautiful*

On a bridge
The view is admired
As the sun rises greeting the sky
The birds fly by
A breeze whispers in your ear
The secrets of the earth.
The wildlife on the hillside
The rocks slide on the mountainside
Admiring its own echo
Imaginations captured by the event
As the moon and stars express themselves
That it may have been forgotten
That something is supporting your wonders
The only way to remember
Is when the bridge timbers
And then you'll wish the bridge was in your priority
When you had the chance...

Sugarcane

"Never let anyone hold the pen to your book"
~ Mom

Sugarcane

Flowers are known for their beauty
But when you go back to the flower's roots
You'll learn they had to grow through the DIRT
To have a beautiful ending

Sugarcane

Silence doesn't mean absence
A room of conversation
The air is full of sound
The one that's quiet
Could be the loudest
Most times,
they're not absent,
they just think louder then they speak.

Sitting on a merry-go-round of denial
The Ferris Wheel of self-defense
The more denial
The faster it loops
The riders will never be able
To get off of the ride
And try something new

The Earth orbits around the Sun
In an everlasting glow
Yesterday is the past
The Earth went around the Sun once
When that happened last
The sorrow of yesterday
Is a whole lap of the Sun Away
No need for *sorrow*
There's always *tomorrow*

Sugarcane

Those that love to climb fences
Yell at others to stop walking the path
That the path walkers enjoy
While they climb their fence
Doing what they enjoy

One Rejects Another
So That One Rejects
Because
They Don't Want To Be
Rejected
Causing The Next To
Reject
It Travels Around The World And Back
Until It Becomes Ice Cold
The Rejected Became The Rejector
The Rejected Made A World Of Rejectors

Sugarcane

Sadness rains from the clouds
Collapse on the ground
Splats at life
But the light still ignites
A smile is in sight
Causing a rainbow of delight

Sugarcane

Snow falls faster then it melts
The blemish of guilt
Kills and spills the emotions it thrills
It calls and falls into a frill
Making it feel impossible to kill
Pay the bill
It melts
The ground will expose the
Green that was covered in snow

You opened the door
And invited me into your home
There was a breeze of delight
Coming through the windows
You gave me a tour
And I explored
Until I found a room that I adored
I stayed there for hours
The breeze from the window
Made me feel so many emotions
It's always a break from the day
I just want to say
Thanks,
To Music

Sugarcane

Expectation deprives the eye
From the best of what it was given
Believing
That the most is what it wants
It can't see that
A blessing is what it was given

An unjust aroma in the air
That is inhaled all of the time
But we became "nose blind"
Through time
The same smell normalizes
The aroma
Until the coma
Of the world
And then
Breathing starts again

Sugarcane

Riding on a horse
Through the flame of winter's breeze
Down the road in summer's anger
Throughout the dropping death of fall
Into the songs of spring
Even when the earth is vexed
Or crying
When it becomes undressed
Or blocking the light of its heart
Sometimes riding becomes unstable
Not considering technology?

Sugarcane

When you are in the fishbowl,
with the other fish,
It's difficult to see your surroundings
But when you are outside of the fishbowl
You can view the entire tank

Authority is in the word
No
It's a self-right
Causing people to respect
You
And for you to respect
Yourself
To say "No" is what you want
To do
But fear sets in
Trapping the word
It can't be heard
When the fear of rejection
Approaches

Remember not to drink the
Alcohol
Of other people's
Opinions,
Actions,
And become intoxicated
With their words
(Lifestyle)
Until your mind is altered
Their opinions become
Your opinion
Their actions become
Your actions
Because it'll never be your
Opinion
It'll be theirs floating
In your high

Sugarcane

The Beauty In The Tree
Started from a seed
Unseen
In the ground, fought through the soil
To make it out
The Beauty Of A Tree
Bikes, metals, can get Stuck
In the trunk
As it grows around
The difficulties
To reach the light above
The Beautiful Tree
Made it through many Things
Through the seasons
It gave itself a reason
To reach its goal
It didn't compare to the Grass
That sits in a group
Unable to reach as high to the sky
No matter how hard it tries
The Power In A Tree
That started as a seed
Sits giant
Peacefully
It stands above all odds
Not easily knocked down
It stands out from the crowd
The Beauty In The Tree

Sugarcane

The row of crumbs into your memory bank
Lead to what is at stake
The actions,
Words,
Emotions,
Of the past
Relive through
Similar gestures,
Phrases,
Feelings,
Of the present
The crumbs lead into your memory bank
Until you feel what you felt in the past
The only way to sweep the crumbs in your brain
Is to come to terms with what happened
Yesterday...

Sitting in a place to see the other side
The lights are so bright that the side
Can not hide
Setting hopes upon a star
To shine as bright
Be the envy of the night
Look deeper into the heart of the side
You'll see what really hides
You'll wish you stayed on your side
Things at night shine brightest in the light

Sugarcane

Lights out
Tables knocked
Walls bumped
No navigation
Feeling stuck
Things on the floor are stomped
Decor overturned
Easily falling
Sitting still is a thought
Darkness Speaking Loud
Overthinking
Who's near or gone
Eventually, the lights turn on...

Sugarcane

The heart was a liquid bliss
Natural cheerfulness
Organically delightful
But then the frost came
And froze the liquid over
Until it was slightly cold

As the white rain arrived
The liquid began to freeze
Until it was solid cold
The liquid bliss
Is now a frozen miss
Because of the weather around it

- They *change with their environment,*
They become their influence.

Words
Are just that
If I scream at a tree to fall
Will it?
If I approach an untrained dog
and demand him to jump
Will he?
If I told a wild bird to follow me
Would she?
If I told my hair to style itself
Would it?
If I commanded a tornado to return to the clouds
Is it?
No
Words are just that
Words have NO physical power
So,
Why are we forced by someone's words
When words can only empower themselves?

Everyone Else Isn't
Me
Everyone Else Isn't
You
Their Opinions Are Theirs
Their Expressions Are Theirs
But Our Feelings Are
Ours
Our Presents Are
Ours
We can choose to leave
We can choose not to let
The words that are theirs
Hurt the feelings
That are ours

There was a turtle
Who saw a bird
And wanted to be
That
He spent his life collecting
Feathers
Hoping to one day have enough
To become a bird
When he collected all of the feathers
He put them on himself thinking he would
Fly
He couldn't
Did he ever really live?

Working hard
Running until your skin begins to drool
Strength used
You can't repair the time
Used
Breathing until your breath is weighted
Running quickly
Confidence thickening
Trapping sense of mind
Becoming blind to the time passing
Running on ice
Towards something that is an
Illusion

Sugarcane

His voice is his power
But his eyes are his mouthpiece
He demands what he wants
He won't rest until he finds
A way to get what he wants
He'll figure it out
His looks are part of his clout
But his heart is gold with no doubt
The inside doesn't match the out
His heart is a sweet golden sprout
His light will never burnout
But through all of the love,
he's the first to turn the lights out.

Sugarcane

Foxes blaming each other

For a forest fire

Life burning down around them

But the only sound they hear

Is the blame of the other

Never a resolve

Nothing solved

But they both burn

In the flames

With no ownership or gain

Never planned to escape

They were busy

Playing the game of

Blame

Sugarcane

The hardest pill to swallow
The largest mountain to climb
Was to realize that
Your reaction
Didn't cause my reaction
Because my reaction
Was still my choice

Naturally Breeding A Dog And Cat
Won't Make A "Cat-Dog"
Naturally Breeding A Deer and Fox
Won't Make A "Deer-Fox"
Though Both of Them Are Healthy
In Their Own Species
They Can't Breed With Something That
They Are Not

-Perfectly Ourselves, But, We aren't alike

Sugarcane

Words,
When you let them in your thoughts
When you wonder if they're true
When it concerns you
Is when it consumes and hurts you

Crossroads:
We ride in our car until
We approach crossroads
One road titled "Happiness"
The other "Unhappiness"
I parked my car
Not to wander too far
Because unhappiness was the first I came too
The gate was opened, awaiting visitors who hoped
To one day leave such sorrow
Next was happiness, locked away, almost hidden
behind a giant lock
I look at my clock, time was not stuck, nor waiting for
me to decide
I peeked inside of unhappiness,
There, everyone searched for the key to happiness
But there was nothing but sorrow on a starless night
I scurried back to my car with a bit of a fright
Because unhappiness won't be the rest of my life
Sitting in my car I glanced upon the stars
Enjoying the things that I have
That's when it hit
I don't have to wonder
What I have, has given me joyous thunder
For the rest of my life, I won't put up a fight,
because I enjoy the things I have in Sight.
Suddenly, the road of happiness opened...

Learned

Honey Crystallizes

The road of life
Is a busy highway
Some people are riding in different lanes,
Others take exits
There are hills, sometimes mountainsides
Flat-roads lead to bridges
Some roads lead to frowns
Others to crowns
The city's sounds
To the country's quiet grounds
Some roads are beautiful
Others deadly
But it's all the road of life

~ Always take a moment
To reevaluate the road you take
You never know when it's time to change lanes
So that you won't accidentally detour in life

Sugarcane

A virus
A cold
The Flu
The immune system
Fights against it
Sending all of its armies to defeat the enemy
Blood cells
Energy
It does whatever it needs to do
To survive
Animals of the wild
Put themselves in danger
To travel and find food
They search
They do whatever they need to do
To survive
It's okay
Express your feelings
Walk away from hateful people
Stay away from harmful people
Never be ashamed of who you are
Listen to your gut
Even if you burn bridges
Do what you have to do
To survive

You make the most delicious honey
It's sweet,
Pure,
Signature,
Special,
But be careful how you treat your honey
Because Bees are the Queens of that
And even they get trapped in their own sap

Sugarcane

Sitting in a class
That no one understands
But no one wants to be the one
To admit that they don't understand
They think that the rest of the class
Will pass
But in reality
No one
Learned from the class
If only someone tried to ask
They would've passed
Pride really is the brick in the bag

Sugarcane

Your destiny
Is farther than the eyes can see
Deeper than ears can hear
Too distant for the skin to touch
People don't believe in it
They can't reach it
Because… it's right in front of
You

Love People
Give to people
Be warm-hearted
Don't let yourself slip in love
Trust in no man
Satan used to be an angel
God himself was disappointed in
People
Don't be saddened, or have expectations
People aren't just hurting you
It's part of nature
It's the evil side of nature
But love is important
Because it conquers hate
If you began to hate
You become the person that hurt
You

Sugarcane

Looking out of the window of an open palace
Peering down on the gardens of sunshine
The family's smiles could be wider then miles
Because happiness is here to stay
The staircase of rubies guides your path
With the mindset that everyone's staircase is of
diamonds
But then a call
And the palace stalls,
As it slowly fades away
Reality sets as you see the rocks in your path
Quiver a river
Beginning to talk until you're done.
I've learned not to trust the lips of one
Whose conversation is only to appeal the listener

What naysayers say
Is the match that lit the fire in your eyes
Its beauty is a disguise
It's the gas that supports your drive
You will achieve and you will survive

Tangled
Detangled
Untangled
A relationship that's forced
No natural remorse
Begins untrue
Ends cursed
Until it gets worse
Uninvolved
Pollution invades the water
They will never be one
Reject things that aren't
As the light in the sun

A group of people who follows
The Leader
A group of people who falls with
Their Leader

Sugarcane

Fear Holds the foot
Stopping it from moving forward
Stress captures the mind
Depriving it from reasoning a way
Of resolve

Don't
Run
From What Hurts
You
To Try and Find Someone
You *Think* Is
Better
Because
If You Haven't <u>Conquered</u>
What Hurt You
You Will
Accidentally
Find Familiar
And Run Into
What You Were Running From
Yes,
It Can Happen
I Watched It Trap Many
Be Careful

Be mindful of those whose
Book has a title that's bold
Enticing to lure
But when you open the book
Your drive will no longer be hooked
Because
The pages are empty

Contrary To Popular Belief
Don't mistreat the people who lived
On the same earth many years longer
One day you too shall be old
Although they haven't grasped
The technology of the new generations
They have already lived through
The base of what we call
The present

Conversation is loud
Behind the wine glass
Within the wineglass speaks the loudest
As it becomes heavy and lightens
And heavy again
You will learn more about the person behind it
Maybe about the person across from it

Reminder-

Most work ends with the sun
That's not the case for everyone
The interior work never seems to be done
Beyond the drum
In your head
The things before you go to bed
What you should've, could've done
Just a reminder to live and have fun.

Patience is Practiced
Conquering Fear is Being Courageous
Love is Learned
Happiness is Having Hope
Being Content Causes Cheerfulness
Gratitude Is Mentally Gaining
Envy is Evil
Fear is Fake
Failing Shouldn't Stop You From Flying

Yes the world is cruel
But becoming like them
Doesn't change the rule
You follow until
You're hollow
Inspire what you want
The world will change
The power of
One
Personal Gain

There's a place
Where there are rainbows without the rain
Perfect delicious tastes
Wonderful Smells in the atmosphere
Confidence everywhere
An amazing world...
Individuality
Greater then words
Strength
A prize
The glow of an angel
A place that is secretly beautiful
It's true
All of this is already inside of
You

Sugarcane

People become blinded by
Light
They can't differ all of the
Colors
In the light
But the colors are present
People underestimate others
Because they can't see
The potential
That's present

Crested Geckos
Drop their tail when they feel threatened
And run away to live a life of freedom
The tail creates a diversion from potential
Predators...
Sometimes
You have to drop something close to you
So that you can continue and be
Free

Be careful of some with
Silent tongues
And
Peaceful eyes
Even cyanide
Lives in a tranquil bottle

I promised
Myself
That I'm going to have more control over
Myself
And not let
Myself
Control
Me
But let me control
Myself
As long as I'm in control over
Myself
I won't let
Myself
Get into the trouble from
My own temptations

The most difficult battle
Was
Teaching my heart
To listen to my mind
When
It sees trouble
While my heart feels mercy

One Sun can brighten the earth
With a drop of glue, two things become one.
One drop of water can ruin a painting
Slipping on one thin sheet of ice
One laugh can change the atmosphere
One drop of color is eye-catching
One pinch of spice changes the flavor
One pepper can burn you
One match can turn a forest into flames
One taste can lure you
One dollar makes $999 turn into $1,000
One drop of bleach changes clothing
One word changes the conversation
One phrase can change a relationship
One event can change a life
One perception changes reality
One experience can change someone's world
One voice can change the world
The
Power
Of
One

- Believe In Yourself

Brick by brick
Layered in metal
Building a wall
Around yourself
To defend yourself
From the war around you
When you finish the wall
You've only trapped yourself
In Yourself
In the middle of a war

Sugarcane

There's beauty in the world
But spending life looking to the left
And not the right
You'll miss half of everything in sight

Perception is
The soul and heart
Of your reality
If you
Remove the soul
You change the appearance
Of your reality
Do not misunderstand
Because your perception
Can cause deception
Making a misconception
Of your reality

A litter of puppies
The breeder striving for all
Black
&
White
But one comes out
With both colors in spots
That's the one they'll
Keep
For being *unique*

Goodness is in one's soul
It fills the heart with happiness
Kindness drips through the pores of their skin
And is revealed through their actions
Be careful of
Transparent venomous snakes
Their kindness is nothing but counterfeit sugar
And is revealed through their actions
Deceit drips through the pores of their skin
It fills the heart with happiness
But, darkness is in their soul

Sugarcane

Swimming in a pond of
Negativity
Choosing either to drown
In it
Or
Swim out of it

Sugarcane

How to capture a moment in a place
So deep your bones will know it…

Search the area with your eyes
Try to copy it into your memory
Then close your eyes,
your camera can also be a distraction.
Smell the air,
let your nostrils taste the moment.
What do you smell?
Let your fingertips feel the climate
Is there an overlooked breeze?
Listen,
inhale the sounds around you with your ears
Deeply suck in the air through your mouth,
into your chest
Cherish the moment,
Fully.
When you reminisce it,
You'll almost relive it.

Enie, Meeny, Miney, Mo
  Struggles come and struggles go
    The strong will still wonder too and fro
      While the weak will sit and *Never* go

Hope
Is Your Goal
Calling You In The Distance
Traveling Through The Wind
Begging, Pleading
For You To Come Closer...

People
Are
Powerful
They have power at the tip of their fingers
But every time they underestimate themselves
They close their OWN power from themselves
(like a fist)
Even though power is in the palm of their hand

Wash your hands
Your hands are
Your **"WILL POWER"**
The dirt on your hands,
Are your past.
The soap is
What encourages you to thrive.
The water,
Time washes away.
Leaving your unwanted memories
Down the drain of the past

Deception:

In order to deceive,
the truth must be told first to gain your trust.
Be cautious of people who tell many truths
They may be slipping a lie in between their points
The best sandwich doesn't hold just one ingredient...
Just because the restaurant claims
"100% beef" doesn't mean the bun itself isn't toxic

Try To Avoid Being A Quick Tempered Person,
Or Being Around Quick Tempered People,
Because:

Anger Lies, And Deceives
It Has No Respect,
It Quickly Consumes Whoever Lets It In
It Blames Others For The Things That It Did
Like A Rose Blaming Me
For The Thrones On Its Stem...

Sugarcane

The Sun
Still finds a way
To brighten the earth on cloudy days
Like perseverance during
Sadness, Disappointment, and *Dismay*

A dangerous group is a group that absentmindedly
follows a leader,
A powerful group is a group that works together with
Independent ideas.
I have yet to meet a group like that... but I dream.

Sometimes doubt screams in my ear
So loud it's hard to bear
My dreams are scared
It's difficult to tell
Rather it's the warning that is real
Or is trying to steal
The fire that I have.
Maybe I've given my last
Doubt blocks the hope and chance
But
Doubt only blocks what is real
It doesn't change what is
It only steals

When something is wanted badly
Eyes open to see
Everyone who has what the eyes are seeking
Destruction of the faith that keeps you awake
When you see your desire
For someone else to admire
Focus on yourself
What you see isn't always reality
Eyes only widen enough to see
What they are searching for

Sugarcane

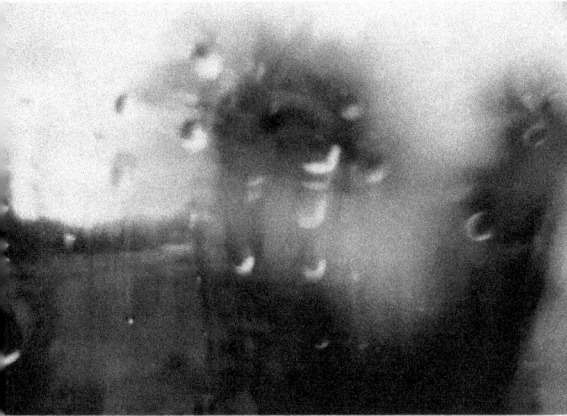

Happiness isn't exchanged in the rain
People forget that we are
One and the same
But the ones who walked through the rain
Cup filled with more than those of the same
They have gain
No reason to envy the ones who skipped
The storm
Because their strength is begging for more
It's easy to give up in the midst of the storm
But then you'll never see the end of what you're
Fighting for

When I was three
I told my mommy
That the devil has a big voice
That's strong and sounds mighty
But he's really just a small thing
With a big voice
People think he's powerful
But in reality
He's just tiny
With a voice that sounds mighty

Fear is a *false* reality
That dwells in the imagination
Becoming vivid
Making itself *seem* like a reality
But in reality, it is only an expectation
Or an expectation that a previous experience
Might be relived
But,
Fear isn't reality
It's a figment of the imagination
Stopping you from exploring the unknown
By imagining the worst possible outcome
Of a situation
That has not entered time itself

A large metal box
Door shut tight
The box shuts out the light
You feel trapped
In a box with sides wrapped
And are carved
With the opinions of others
Touch one side, you feel judged
Touch another side, you're not excepted
Back to the middle of the box
Trying not to be judged by the walls
You forget that the power to escape
Was always with you
Push open the door
You are free
To be who you want to be

Sugarcane

Worrying
About what she couldn't control
Was only a distraction
From changing
What she could control

~ Distracted from an opportunity

People,
Like an animal in the yard
Won't change for opinions
Doesn't change for suggestions
Only changes when they decide too
It's impossible to change another being
Unless they decide to change themselves
Emotions like a ray of light
On a situation
Might
Help
But won't be the only thing to change
Another
Worrying about the change
That doesn't want to change
The refusal of the changing
Is a waste of time to the changer

Sugarcane

There is a wave in the air
That kills the kindness of most
It cuts throats, vinegar in their eye
No surprise it walks too a fro
It makes you trust
Then lets you go
It causes mistrust in the victim
Making the victim become the suspect
In the next case
There is a wave in the air
That preys on the innocent
When they need it the most.
Is it time to let them go?
Heartbreak?
The energy for the body comes from the heart
Break the heart, murder the heart
Now they have control
Let them go
They'll become just like the murderer
And now, the globe is cold
It claimed the warm hearts
Then lets them go
In order to stand against the serial killings
You must stand against the wave
Yes it hurts, but it works
If you win
You'll start the change that needs
To Get In

What happened in the past
Remains there
Becoming the
Toxic
Potion
Of emotions
You
Remain living in what you hate
Staying away from what you want
Punishing yourself
For what
They've done

Sugarcane

The silence of the woods
The crackle of my steps as I run
The sun
Beams through the trees
As the breeze whispers with ease
Steps in search of something deep
Something different than the norm
I realize I'm going in the same circle as before
I'm already in what I'm searching for

Sugarcane

Instead of chasing people
I met this new girl,
I like her a lot
She's honest with me
She was always here but
I didn't appreciate her
She. Is. Me.

New Chapter

*Seasons Later,
Honey Never Spoiled*

"The Little Girl Never Knew,
The Power,
In The Breath She Blew."

The warm, sweet, tender
Love
From someone who
Decided to keep it
Can melt ice off of the coldest
Soul
Love is powerful
It conquers all
But society disrespects it
So that the power won't be used
Hate knows it can be defeated
So it speaks louder than Love
But Love can still win
Silently

Sugarcane

Loving the way he walks
It captures my eye
Appealing my heart
Grasps my emotions
My hopes are set high
I would never say goodbye
To your walk in my eyes

Sugarcane

The power on the inside
Keeping information
Using information
Smaller than the human body
But
Can outsmart multitudes
Never underestimate your mind

Change the color of the light
Its surroundings change color also
Your surroundings become
Who you are
You become what you are surrounded
With
Changing my surroundings from
Dark
To
Light
I've become happier at night

Sugarcane

My heart can quickly love what
You are
Hope for
What you could be
Drown in the words you speak
Fall in love with who you show me
But stop listening to sounds I hear
When you tell me,
Show me
Who you really are.
My mind has learned
To watch and
Listen
When they tell me who they are

Sugarcane

The more people I meet
I've found
That everyone seems to have a little
Hurt they hide
They deprive from seeing the light
Not to sound like it's a prize of a find
But it feels better on the inside
That I'm not the only one
Who was hurt from time to time

Sugarcane

I was hiding behind the sign that states
"I'm Fine"
Wrapped my emotions and pride
To keep safe on the inside
In hope that eventually
Someone else
Will come wrapped in love
To open the gift
I wished to find
My solace in whoever unlocks the code I set
I realized that I'm holding the code
To the lock I set
I must invest in myself
So that I can unlock my own
If I unlock myself I'll never leave myself
If I leave it up to someone else
They will choose to lock and unlock me
As THEY please
My Life Would No Longer Be Up To Me

The house of beauty
The house of wonder
The house of life
Where hope dwells
Families are thriving here
Don't take the house for granted
It will
Fall apart
Repair the house as needed
Cherish what is in it
Keep the house alive
It'll thrive
And so will you

The paint of your thoughts
The paintbrush of your lips
Paints the canvas of your life
Painting with negative colors
The canvas will mirror your feelings
Paint with positivity
The canvas will brighten your world

I felt a void within myself
Like my heart was missing
Out of my chest
I could never fill the void in other people
Because they didn't put the void there
The void came when you left
Or
I left myself when you left
The only way to fill a void is to
Fill it with yourself
When you are whole
With yourself
The void can not be made
By no one else

Sugarcane

Sometimes,
The person in the mirror is who you need
Let your reflection speak the truth in your
Reality
Tell yourself how strong you are
Encourage yourself
Don't let yourself fail
The only way you can fail
Is when you give up on your goal
Because it's the only way the goal
Will never be completed

-Reminder

Tell the people you care about
How much you love them
Encourage them
Let them know how you feel
Don't ever make them wonder
To keep a relationship shining bright
You'll have to keep replacing
The lightbulb

Sugarcane

When you take time
You'll enjoy the small things
Like tender kisses of the breeze
The breeze is peaceful
It's kind
It lightly massages your skin
Like kisses from the earth
It speaks, it whispers
Soothing things
It gives you the kindest hug
Just enough to prove its presence
But also its distance

Sugarcane

The earth always speaks
But people don't stop
To listen

Sugarcane

In order to dig a tunnel
You'll have to disturb the dirt
In order to paint a picture
You have to put color on a flawless canvas
In order to change the world
You have to come out of
Your comfort zone

Sugarcane

Noticing the
technology in the air,
the light shines
bright.
I refuse
To be blinded by the
light,
That I become
blinded
to what's happening
around me.
Once you are
blinded
one day you may
look to see,
and notice
that you are blinded
from the
importance
of the change that's
happening around
You
But then it'll be too late

Walking on a path on a mountain
To your goal
There are flowers down below
The view of beauty captures your desire
Don't wander off the path
To look at the view
It's easy to slip
Off of the side of a cliff
The fall
Is painful
-Stay On Your Path

Choose your battles wisely,
Sometimes the enemy
Gives you false battles
To tire out your army
So that you won't be able to
Fight the real battle

Sugarcane

Time runs away and
Never comes back
Time wasted on making
Time
For people that don't make time
For you
Is a waste of time

To conquer the fear
Of the outdoors
You'll have to go outside
To conquer the fear of the dark
You'll have to turn out the lights
To conquer any fear in life
You have to
Do what you fear
So that you can move forward

"Deciding not to be a balloon anymore."
The balloon flies high
Without a destiny
It floats, being guided by the wind
It constantly shifts
It's delicate, it suddenly
Pops
When there's a
Change on the
Track of its train.
I decided to be an Eagle
Who flies into high altitudes
A destination is a reason why she soars
Who uses the wind to glide
Who fights for what she wants
They don't try to mix with
Flocks of other birds
They know who they are
They are confident in it

It's okay not to be perfect
We are all just bottles of wine
We get better as time goes by
Take care of yourself
Try not to be the few wines
That go bad after time

Sugarcane

Being a sour sap of unhappiness
Only left me in the trap
Feeling,
Living,
In my past
I won't get past
Until I turn
My sour
Sweet

- Happiness Is My Choice,
Honey

Where are the guidelines?
Where are the measurements?
Between "weird" and "normal"
Between "ugly" and "pretty"
Between "fat" and "thin"
Between "perfect" and "imperfect"
Who made the guidelines?
Between "Body Envy" and "Body Embarrassment"
Between "Too Dark" and "Too Pale"
Between "Too Short" and "Too Tall"
Where is the crossover?
Between how to be,
How to act,
How to look,
Before there was someone's personal preference
That was *mentally made up*
Because we can't define beauty using words
We can't define color using words
To someone who could never
See
Before there were enough people to choose
If no one told us what "pretty" should be,
Would it still be pretty?
If no one said what "normal" is
Would it still be normal?
What is Truth?

There's darkness in-between
The sunset and the sunrise
Where the sins of the night
Arise
The coldest time
But then the sunrise
Beauty laced with love
From the above
If the sunrise was the regular sky
It would cause boring eyes
But
Because of the darkest night
The eyes appreciate the
Sunrise

Sometimes my inner being
Is screaming
Telling me to start fleeing
I listen to my inner being
It sees what I am not seeing
Reading farther
Then I am reading
Listen to the inner being
Even if you aren't believing
When push comes to shove
You're not walking into love

Seeing your goal in the distance
Walking through the earth's seasons
Giving
Reasons to quit
When it gets hard
Walk
When doubt arrives
Jog
When Quitting is near
Run
Towards the goal

The actions of another
Are not my own
Why travel a journey to *change* what is
Not me
Why be affected by words that are
Not mine
Dreams that I don't imagine
People that aren't in the same passion
Bridges that I won't cross
To rock a boat
To sink a moat
Or
To keep things afloat?

- Reminding Myself Not To Change For Others

Sugarcane

Walking
With a fence by my side
What would it profit
To worry about the maintenance of the
Fence
If it isn't blocking my path

Honey Pot, Honey Pot
How will you fill?
Be aloof from She
Who eats your properties
Just to find a new pot to devour
Leaving you without power.
Honey Pot, Honey Pot
How Will You End?
Stay Weary Of Him
Who fills your pot
Just to crack the bottom
Leaving you emptying
And ending with sorrow/
Honey Pot, Honey Pot
What does you well?
Fill yourself with delicious delight
Leaving no room for thieves to steal
Find someone who's just as full
And you will be each others tool
To remain filled

Sugarcane

Those with thrones in their mouths
Tongues of fire
Paths of burdens.
Remembering not to be afraid
To let go of those
Whose fingertips are of disorder
Whose intentions aren't pure
The weight of the wary
Is too heavy to hold

Sugarcane

She stopped
Going down the same
Road
Searching for a new
Destination

She Is the Hero
She Needed
She Is Who She Craved
She Never Knew It
Until She Really Needed
Herself

A town of people
Who hide their imperfections with
Masks
Each *believing* the masks they are
Seeing
Trying to be the perfect version of
Themselves to cope
In hope
Of dreaming and being the perfection
They're seeing
The happiest knows
Behind the masks and the laughs
No one is really perfect
Happiness dwells in the
Acceptance of your natural self
And the commitment to still better yourself
While being yourself

Sugarcane

She learned that
Self-love
Is the sweetest,
Kindest,
Love to have
Sometimes
It's the hardest love the find
But it's an important love
To feel
And to
To keep

Thinking,
Overthinking,
Reimagining,
The moment
Only causing
Me
To relive the
Place
I don't want to be

-So I Stopped Doing That

Two colors mixed together
Creates a color that's
Unrecognizable
Going out of your way
To be accepted
By a group
Creates a person that's
Unrecognizable

- I Stopped Doing That, Too

Sugarcane

Telling millions to
Stay away from abuse
Trying to avoid abusive relationships
What does it profit
When we are in an abusive relationship
With ourselves?

- No more doubting myself
No more talking bad about myself
To myself
No more excuses
No more

(I have to be my biggest supporter)

I try not to waste time
At the end we waste time
Wasting more time
Worrying about how much time
We wasted
But
Details are missed
In the time that is
Rushed

Sugarcane

Keep fighting
Don't look back
That's time spent
Not viewing your track
Even when something tries
To hold you back
Never stop the fight
You'll Eventually Shine Bright

Sugarcane

Lies flying in the sky
Blocking the light
Making life seem like night
Don't let the clouds
Block the hope you have
The faith you've grabbed
The light is still there
No matter what people say

Sugarcane

Believing you've read a book
Without reading it
Believing you've done something
Without doing it
Believing something
That you've never seen or experienced
Judging A Person
Believing you know them
Without knowing them

Honey Drips
Honey Drops
Honey is Sweet
It sits in its spot
But
Honey is powerful
Benefits are valuable
Underestimated
It sits in the pot
Aging in crystals
Strength of pistols
The silent, motionless sap
Trapped, sealed with a cap
Knows what to do
It could save multitudes

I've Learned
And
Live On
The fact that
In Order To Stay On Track
And Not Circle In Life
I Always Have To Reexamine The Route
I'm Traveling
Rethink The Company
I Keep
Reconsider My
Personal Opinion
Reevaluate The Life
I'm Living
And
Continue
To Better Myself
For Myself

The bees that **sting** are
Attracted to my *honey*
But it's okay
They also <u>make</u> the *honey*
The more they pile in my hive
I'm learning new ways to rhyme
Feeling stronger
The *honey* spills over
Though the bees sting and die
I have a bigger hive
Lessons learned
Conquered
Power arrived
All because of the bees
That makes the *honey* in my
Hive

Sugarcane

The most empowering moment in life
Is when you climb
Through the growl of the wind,
and the anger in the storm.
When you endured the surprises,
That almost knocked you down.
When you recovered from the
Deadly intentions of an avalanche.
When you prove everyone wrong
Because you're still thriving,
And you've finally made it to the top
Of the mountain.
The most empowering moment in life
Is when you look down
And see where you've come from,
While witnessing the beauty of where you are.

Thank you
For reading my storytime
I became Sugarcane
When I conquered the sour phase
But chose to still be sweet.
I fought for the nectar in my eyes
When I could still see the beautiful side
Of what is around me.
The honey in my veins
Is the happiness I've claimed
From the lessons of learned
From my recent stage.
I keep my seasons by my side
Not to sigh,
But to keep insight
To remember what not to do
To remind myself the strength gained
To break all of life's chains.

I hope I've inspired you,
to *realize* the *strength you have.*
I hope you know
you're not alone, in whatever you're going through.
You have potential, please
Don't Ever Give Up.
I hope you never settle for less
Please don't look to your past,
you're moving toward your future.
Words only empower themselves.

Love yourself,
Better yourself,
Be yourself,
Love others,
No expectations.
Don't become what you hated
Never give up and miss out on your dream
that will come true
Don't underestimate yourself
Face your fear.

If you trip on a rock in your path
Get up and keep working
Keep fighting for your goals
You are important
You are worth more than you know

Give love, because the more love you give
The more your honey pot fills
The more love you feel
When love becomes a habit
You'll love yourself as well
See love from your view
But be careful don't be fooled
Guard your heart
But remain
Love Filled.

Most importantly,
"Never Let Anyone Have The Pen
To Your Book"

- Mom -

John 3:16

www.ingramcontent.com/pod-product-compliance
Lightning Source LLC
Chambersburg PA
CBHW051824040426
42447CB00006B/353